j383
RUS

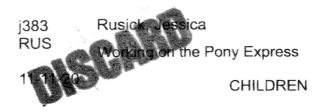

Rusick, Jessica

Working on the Pony Express

11-11-20

CHILDREN

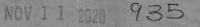

THIS OR THAT? *History Edition*

Working on the PONY EXPRESS

A This or That Debate

by Jessica Rusick

CAPSTONE PRESS
a capstone imprint

Capstone Captivate is published by Capstone Press, an imprint of Capstone.
1710 Roe Crest Drive
North Mankato, Minnesota 56003
www.capstonepub.com

Library of Congress Cataloging-in-Publication Data is available on the Library of Congress website.
ISBN: 978-1-4966-8393-9 (library binding)
ISBN: 978-1-4966-8791-3 (paperback)
ISBN: 978-1-4966-8444-8 (eBook PDF)

Summary: In 1860 and 1861, riders on horseback delivered mail across the United States for the Pony Express. Test your decision-making skills with this or that questions related to working for this historic mail service!

Image Credits
Flickr: British Library, 6, Bureau of Land Management, 17, 24, Internet Archive Book Images, 13, Public Lands History Center, 19; iStockphoto: mppriv, 11; Library of Congress: John M. Atwood, Cover (map); Shutterstock: alexkich, 21, Anneka, Cover (old letters), Branding Pot, 3, Bryan Chernick, Cover (mountains), CD_Photography, 14, Charlie Bird, 7, Dominic Gentilcore PhD, 23, Everett Historical, 16, Jiri Prochazka, 9, John D Sirlin, 27, knelson20, 25, Lesleyanne Ryan, 26, mariait, 8, Mariusz S. Jurgielewicz, Cover (statue), Marsan, 15, Michael Roeder, 29, Neil Lockhart, 10, OsbornRiverRanch, 28, Ricardo Reitmeyer, 22, Sascha Burkard, 18, Seita, 12, YK, Cover (horse), Zoran Milic, 5 (map); Wikimedia Commons: Federal Highway Administration, 4–5, Pony Express, 30, William Henry Jackson, 20

Design Elements: John M. Atwood/Library of Congress

Editorial Credits
Editor: Rebecca Felix; Designers: Aruna Rangarajan & Tamara JM Peterson; Production Specialist: Tori Abraham

All internet sites appearing in back matter were available and accurate when this book was sent to press.

Printed in the United States of America.
PA117

EXPRESS MAIL

The Pony Express mail delivery service started in April 1860. Riders rode horses to deliver mail from Missouri to California. They traveled 1,800 miles (2,900 kilometers) in 10 days. This was much shorter than the 25 days delivery by **stagecoach** took.

The Pony Express route had stations. Riders changed horses every 10 to 15 miles (16 to 24 km) at a station. Riders faced bad weather, accidents, and exhaustion.

In October 1861, a **telegraph** line connected the east and west. Messages could be wired across the country almost instantly. This meant the end of the Pony Express.

HOW TO USE THIS BOOK

What if you had worked on the Pony Express? What choices would you have made? Do you think you would have survived?

This book is full of questions that relate to the Pony Express. Some are questions real people had to face. The questions are followed by details to help you come to a decision.

THE PONY EXPRESS ROUTE

California

Missouri

KEY

Trail

N
W E
S

Pick one choice or the other. There are no wrong answers! But just like the riders and other workers, you should think carefully about your decisions.

Are you ready? Turn the page to pick this or that!

Would you choose . . .

THIS

To work as a

RIDER?

➤ face constant danger

➤ exhausting

➤ often without comfortable place to rest

Riding for the Pony Express was dangerous. Riders had to deliver the mail no matter what. They traveled through rain and snowstorms. They could be thrown from their horses or lose their way. Riders rested at buildings called home stations. Some were like nice hotels. But many others had only simple beds and spoiled food to eat.

To work at a
RELAY STATION?

➤ dirty conditions

➤ cramped living space

➤ must defend station if it
   is attacked

Riders changed horses at relay stations. Usually, a relay station had only two workers. They kept track of arrivals and cared for horses. Relay stations often had one room and little furniture. Some had dirt floors. Many stations were built in **remote** areas. That meant there was no one around to help if the workers got injured or attacked by **thieves**.

THIS

To ride a
HORSE?

> ➤ very fast
>
> ➤ could be too eager
>
> ➤ could get injured on rocks

Most Pony Express riders rode horses. Horses covered long distances quickly and could outrun most dangers. However, they sometimes had trouble walking over rocks. The horses were also energetic and focused—even to a fault. Once, a horse carried mail by itself to the next station after its rider was too slow to mount it!

To ride a
MULE?

➤ better for riding on rocky land

➤ not as fast as horses

➤ can have bad attitudes

Mules were less common than horses on the Pony Express. Mules are smaller than horses and better for mountain travel. A mule's feet and legs are stronger than a horse's. However, mules are slower than horses. They had a harder time outrunning danger. Mules are also **stubborn**. An angry mule might refuse to move.

THIS

To BUILD A RELAY STATION in the desert?

- ➤ must work in the hot sun
- ➤ messy work
- ➤ hard labor

Relay stations in the east were often set up in existing buildings. Out west, Pony Express organizers had to build stations. Some were built in the hot, dry desert and made from **adobe**. Making adobe was a messy process. Workers formed mud bricks out of sand, clay, or straw and waited for them to dry. Then they put the bricks together.

To DELIVER SUPPLIES to a desert relay station?

➤ must travel across hot, dry land

➤ slow process to pull a heavy wagon

➤ danger of being stranded

Pony Express organizers tried to build relay stations near water sources. However, this was not always possible. Some stations had to have water and supplies delivered by wagon. Even a short wagon journey in the desert could be dangerous. People could suffer weakness from heat and lack of water. Any wagon accidents meant the party would be stranded.

THIS

To ride a horse through a HEAT WAVE?

➤ must drink lots of water to stay hydrated

➤ could get heat stroke

➤ hard to stay on horse

Parts of the Pony Express route crossed desert. In the desert heat, riders and horses could become dehydrated. Dehydration happens when the body does not get enough water. It can make you tired and dizzy. This would make it hard to ride a horse. The heat could also give a rider **heatstroke**. Heat stroke causes weakness and headache. If heat stroke is left untreated, it can lead to death.

To ride a horse through a
SNOWSTORM?

➤ could get lost

➤ body temperature could drop too low

➤ hard to stay on horse

Riders also traveled through snowstorms. In a storm, they could lose the trail. Riders who spent too long in the cold could also get hypothermia. This happens when a person's body temperature is too low. Hypothermia makes people feel weak and sleepy. One lost rider almost froze to death after falling asleep in a snowstorm.

Would you choose . . .

THIS

To experience EXHAUSTION during a trip?

- ➤ could fall asleep while riding
- ➤ could become injured if you fall off your horse
- ➤ if you stop to rest, you could make the mail late

Riders were not supposed to rest before reaching their home station. Exhausted riders sometimes fell asleep in their saddles. This put them at great risk of falling off their horses. A rider's time was tracked at each station. So station workers knew which rider made the mail late, damaging the Pony Express commitment to speedy delivery.

To experience FOOD POISONING AND DIARRHEA during a trip?

> comes from eating bad food

> could become weak while riding

> if you stop to get relief, you could make the mail late

Many home stations in remote areas did not have access to good food. Riders who ate bad food could get sick with **vomiting** and **diarrhea**. This would make them weak and dizzy, making it difficult to stay on a horse. But stopping to get relief meant making the mail late.

THIS

To LEAVE THE PONY EXPRESS *after a few months?*

> leave behind hardships of job

> lose out on good paycheck

> lose out on adventure

Most Pony Express riders quit after a few months. They were exhausted and did not like how lonely the job was. Quitting meant leaving these hardships behind. It also meant losing money. Riders made up to $150 a month. That's $4,236 in today's money. This was a great wage for the time. Those who left were unlikely to make as much money somewhere else.

To **KEEP RIDING** for its entirety?

> riding for longer makes your body sore

> stress of facing danger

> earn more money

Some riders worked for the Pony Express until it went out of business. They spent more time riding horses, which could make them sore and tired. They also spent more time facing stressful dangers like bad weather and accidents. However, these riders continued to earn high pay for their work.

THIS

To REFUSE TO RIDE
when there are known dangers in the area?

➤ stay safe

➤ face anger from other riders

➤ could lose your job

Some riders refused to ride when thieves were in the area. They would not take over from another rider when they were supposed to. Refusing to ride meant you wouldn't be killed or injured. However, fellow riders might call you a **coward**. You would also go against the **oath** Pony Express riders had to take. This meant you could lose your job.

To RIDE INTO KNOWN DANGER?

➤ risk your life

➤ carry out the oath you took

➤ might get bonus pay

W. H. JACKSON

Other riders chose to ride in dangerous conditions. This put them at greater risk of being killed if they crossed paths with thieves. Some riders carried weapons like rifles. But these added extra weight, so many riders chose to go without. Riders who completed dangerous trips were sometimes given extra money.

Would you choose . . .

THIS

To LOSE YOUR MOCHILA?

- ➤ riders must keep their mochilas safe at all costs

- ➤ only one mochila was ever lost, so it would be shameful to lose yours

- ➤ could be fired

The success of the Pony Express depended on mail being delivered quickly and safely. Riders carried mail in a **mochila** that they were expected to keep safe, even if it meant risking their lives. Riders saved mochilas from flooded rivers and other dangers. Only one Pony Express mochila was ever lost. A rider who lost a mochila could be fired.

To **LOSE YOUR HORSE?**

➤ must walk rest of route

➤ hard to outrun danger without horse

➤ must carry your heavy mochila

Horses sometimes got injured or exhausted on the route. If this happened, a rider would have to leave his horse and walk to the next station. This walk could be more than 10 miles (16 km)! Without a horse, a rider wouldn't be able to outrun thieves or wild animals. Riders also had to carry their mochilas. These could weigh up to 20 pounds (9 kilograms).

THIS

To ride through the
GREAT PLAINS?

- ➤ very hot during summer
- ➤ harsh winter snowstorms
- ➤ crowded in summer, so have to avoid more obstacles

The first part of the route went through the Great Plains. This land is west of the Mississippi River and east of the Rocky Mountains. The Great Plains saw harsh snowstorms in the winter. Summers in the Great Plains were very hot. During this time, the area also became crowded with travelers heading west. A rider would have to dodge wagons, trash, and dead animals.

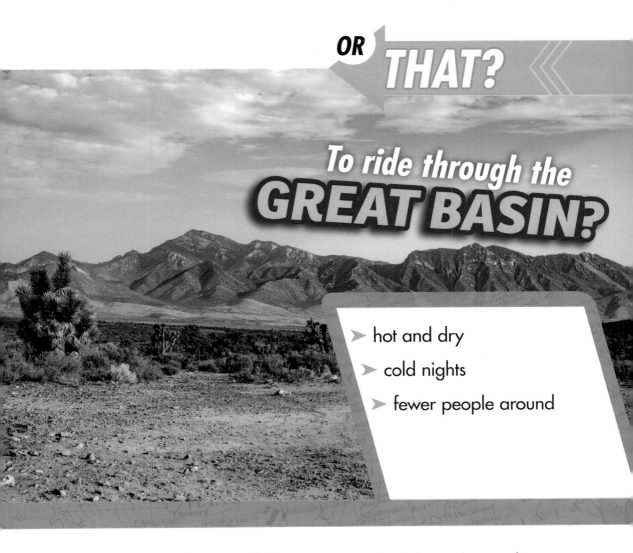

To ride through the
GREAT BASIN?

➤ hot and dry

➤ cold nights

➤ fewer people around

The second part of the route took riders through the Great Basin. This includes parts of California, Utah, Idaho, Oregon, Wyoming, and Nevada. Days were hot. However, even during summer, nights were cold. Wagon trails usually avoided the Great Basin. This meant the route wouldn't be crowded. However, riders faced unknown dangers by riding in a less traveled area.

THIS

To SURVEY
where to build relay stations?

- ➤ involves traveling through different types of dangerous land
- ➤ land not well known
- ➤ could get lost

Surveyors had to find the straightest, fastest path for the Pony Express. They chose where to build relay stations. Much of the route followed the path settlers used to go west. However, the last portion did not. Surveyors traveled over mountains, deserts, and rivers to plot the best route. These areas were not well known. If surveyors weren't careful, they could get lost.

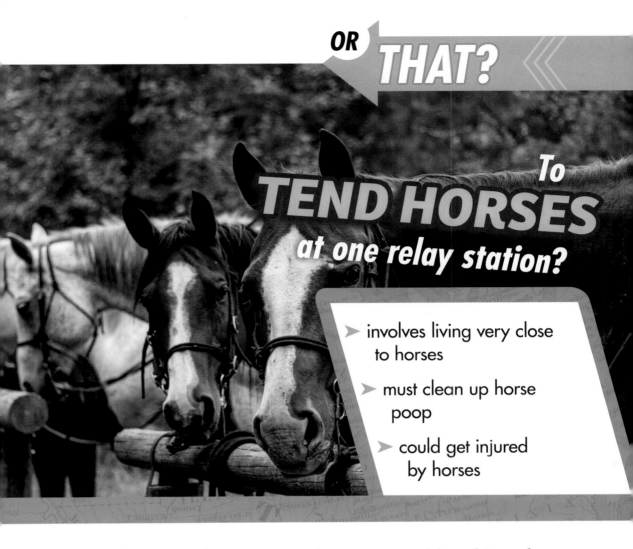

To TEND HORSES at one relay station?

➤ involves living very close to horses

➤ must clean up horse poop

➤ could get injured by horses

Workers at relay stations slept, ate, and lived just feet away from the station's horses. They were responsible for keeping the animals healthy and ready to ride. This meant cleaning up smelly horse poop. It also meant keeping the animals clean and well fed. Workers were always at risk of being stepped on or kicked by the horses.

THIS

To ride in a
RAINSTORM?

➤ your horse could slip and fall in mud

➤ clothes will get wet and uncomfortable

➤ might have to cross flooded streams

Rain made the route muddy and dangerous. Horses could slip and fall in mud, injuring both themselves and their riders. Riders might have to cross flooded streams. If the water was too deep, they could get swept away. Riders only had about two minutes to change horses at relay stations. There was no time to change into dry clothes.

To ride in a DUST STORM?

- could lose the trail
- hard to breathe
- grains of dust are painful when hitting skin at high speeds

Dust storms made it hard for riders to see. They could lose their way and wander for hours. Tiny grains of dust pelted any exposed skin. Dust could also make it hard to breathe. Riders had only **bandannas** to cover their noses and mouths. They were not supposed to stop due to weather. Even in a dust storm, riders had to keep going.

To face a
BUFFALO HERD?

> ➤ a large herd can block your route

> ➤ easy to spot from far away

> ➤ can scare horses and trample riders who fall off their horses

Some areas along the route were home to large herds of buffalo. There could be thousands of animals in a herd! Herds could block a rider's way. It was dangerous to ride through a herd. Buffalo could scare a rider's horse, causing the rider to fall off and get trampled. A horse could also scare the buffalo, causing the buffalo to **stampede**.

To face a
WOLF PACK?

> can scare horses

> may chase after horses and riders

> could bite

Wolf packs were also a danger. Unlike buffalo, wolves chased after riders and horses. If riders weren't careful, they could get bitten. The wolves could also scare horses. A scared horse can cause its rider to fall off, possibly causing injury. One rider used a horn to scare off a hungry wolf pack.

LIGHTNING ROUND

Would you choose to . . .

➤ receive extra money or a gold watch as a prize for delivering mail in record time?

➤ read a book or play cards to pass time while working at a relay station?

➤ eat cured meat or dried fruit as a snack at a relay station?

➤ encounter wild animals or thieves?

➤ ride with a twisted ankle or sprained wrist?

➤ lose your water pack or weapon during a ride?

➤ eat spoiled antelope meat or drink milk with flies in it?

➤ be in charge of buying horses or hiring riders for the Pony Express?

GLOSSARY

adobe (uh-DOH-bee)—bricks made of clay mixed with straw and dried in the sun

bandanna (ban-DAN-uh)—a large square of fabric, usually worn around the head or neck

coward (KOU-urd)—a person who lacks the courage to face unpleasant or dangerous situations

diarrhea (dye-uh-REE-uh)—a condition in which normally solid waste from your body becomes liquid

heatstroke (HEET-strohk)—a life-threatening condition that results from prolonged exposure to high temperature

mochila (mo-CHEE-la)—a square leather saddle covering often equipped with saddlebags

oath (OHTH)—a formal promise or declaration

remote (ri-MOHT)—far away, secluded, or isolated

stagecoach (STAYJ-kohch)—a four-wheeled, horse-drawn coach

stampede (stam-PEED)—a sudden, wild rush in one direction, usually out of fear

stubborn (STUHB-urn)—not willing to give in or change

telegraph (TEL-i-graf)—a device or system for sending messages over long distances using electrical signals sent by wire or radio

thief (THEEF)—a person who steals others' belongings or money

vomit (VAH-mit)—to bring up food from the stomach and expel it through the mouth

READ MORE

Bougie, Matt. *Life as a Pony Express Rider in the Wild West.*
New York: Cavendish Square Publishing, 2018.

Faust, Daniel R. *The Real Story Behind the Wild West.*
New York: PowerKids Press, 2020.

Quiri, Patricia R. *The Groundbreaking Pony Express.*
North Mankato, MN: Capstone Press, 2018.

INTERNET SITES

Ducksters—Westward Expansion: Pony Express
https://www.ducksters.com/history/westward_expansion/pony
_express.php

National Pony Express Association—Here Comes the Pony!
https://nationalponyexpress.org/

Pony Express National Historic Trail—Long Distance Communication
https://www.nps.gov/poex/index.htm